THE ASTONISHI

WEIGHT OF THE DE

TOM WAYMAN

for Stu —
with many thanks!

Tom Wayman

12/9 4

WAYMAN,
TOM

THE ASTONISHING WEIGHT OF THE DEAD

The Astonishing Weight of the Dead

Published by:
Polestar Press Ltd.
1011 Commercial Drive, Second Floor
Vancouver, BC
Canada   V5L 3X1

The publisher would like to thank the Canada Council, the British Columbia Ministry of Small Business, Tourism and Culture, and the Department of Canadian Heritage for their ongoing financial assistance.

Cover photograph by Jeremy Addington
Cover design by Jim Brennan
Editing by Julian Ross
Production by Michelle Benjamin and Julian Ross
Printed in Canada by Best Book Manufacturers

Canadian Cataloguing in Publication Data

Wayman, Tom, 1945-
   The astonishing weight of the dead

Poems.
ISBN 0-919591-08-6
   I. Title.
PS8595.A9A87 1994 C811'.54 C94-910610-0
PR9199.3W39A87 1994

ACKNOWLEDGEMENTS

I very much appreciate the support of the editors who published or accepted for publication poems from this volume in the magazines: *Border/Lines, Caliban, The Canadian Forum, Canadian Literature, Colorado Review, Education Forum, Event, The Fiddlehead, The Fisherman, 5 A.M., Left Bank, The Malahat Review, North Dakota Quarterly, Ontario Review, Our Schools/Our Selves, Poetry Canada, Poetry East, Poetry Northwest, Prairie Fire, Prism international, Processed World, Quarry, Queen's Quarterly, Saturday Night, This Magazine, W Magazine*; "Country Incomplete," "Fire Elegy," "The Heart Is Also a Meadow," and "Waley, Waley" were first published in *The Hudson Review*; "The Iceberg, the Shadow" first appeared in *TriQuarterly*, a publication of Northwestern University. As well, poems here appeared in the anthologies *Barbed Lyres, East of Main: An Anthology of Poems from East Vancouver, Inside the Poem, More Than Our Jobs*, and *Words We Call Home*.

Some details of natural history in "Mountain Elegy" are taken from the excellent essays of R.W. Sandford of Canmore, Alberta.

This book is in memory of: Dave Bostock, Leo Clavir, Dave Forsythe, Henrietta Geller, Beryl Lowry, Mary Rapson, Bron Wallace.

Love and awe and incalculable thanks to Heather Chrisara, for her wisdom and dancing through dark times and light.

And this book is for John Lent.

Other books by Tom Wayman

Poetry:

Waiting For Wayman   1973
For and Against the Moon: Blues, Yells and Chuckles   1974
Money and Rain: Tom Wayman Live!   1975
Free Time   1977
A Planet Mostly Sea   1979
Living on the Ground: Tom Wayman Country   1980
Introducing Tom Wayman   1980 (USA)
The Nobel Prize Acceptance Speech   1981
Counting the Hours: City Poems   1983
The Face of Jack Munro   1986
In a Small House on the Outskirts of Heaven   1989
Did I Miss Anything? Selected Poems 1973-1993   1993

Essays:

Inside Job: Essays on the New Work Writing   1983
A Country Not Considered: Canada, Culture, Work   1993

Editor:

Beaton Abbot's Got the Contract   1974
A Government Job at Last   1976
Going for Coffee   1981
East of Main (with Calvin Wharton)   1989
Paperwork   1991

THE ASTONISHING WEIGHT OF THE DEAD

CABIN NEWS

HEART MOUNTAIN

CARGO

HOW I BECAME A PLANET

THE POLITICS OF THE HOUSE

SOME RANTS

X-RATED

THE WINLAW ELEGIES

CABIN NEWS

WOMAN WHO CALLS HORSES

On a Valley road, I saw
through the dusk, a figure in a white dress
hovering in a field whose green
had nearly all been drained.
She stared past a deep gully
toward a far part of the pasture
where it seemed white horses grazed.
And I heard her
whinny,
the sound carried to me
above the steady thin grinding
of crickets
under a half moon. As I watched
she whinnied again,
raising and lowering her outstretched arms
but nothing happened.
                                    And then the faintest
tremor in the earth
like distant thunder
growling, then hoofbeats,
then out of the night
the spectral face
of a white horse running,
then another, five in all
closing the distance toward her
as she ran back toward the fence
then turned, standing her ground,
the horses cantering to a stop
churning around her, hoofs and manes,
her white clothes,
their white hair,
her hand now on one's nose
now another's flank,
as they shifted and jostled
surrounding her
                          until one

spun about
and began trotting
back to the darkness
and then a second, then
the small herd was receding, galloping
into sound
and then only the crickets' drone.

And I heard
the woman laugh, a wild
night laugh
of fierceness
and pleasure
and dread

THE MAN WHO LOGGED THE WEST RIDGE

The man who logged the West Ridge,
unlike the person who owns it,
has his home on the Valley floor.
The money this man got
for taking away the West Ridge's trees
paid a crew, made payments on a truck
and a skidder, reduced a mortgage, bought food
and a new outboard
and was mailed off to the owner.

So the fir and larch and pine
of the Ridge, its deer and coyote,
snails and hummingbirds,
were dollars for a brief time,
then were gone from our Valley.
Fair enough. While the logging was in progress
the man stood on the new road along the slope
to shout at a pickup full of people from below
over the howls of the saws
and the surging diesels:
I don't have to talk to you.
I am leaving a few trees. I don't have to do that.
Bug me, and I'll level this place completely.

Once the West Ridge was empty,
the owner put the land up for sale.
Remaining that close to the sky
is slash, and the churned soil,
heaps of cable and plastic oil containers
and a magazine of photographs
of young women's breasts and vaginas
that got passed around one lunchhour
and looked at, while everyone ate their sandwiches
resting against some logs. Nobody wanted to keep
the publication, not even the one who brought it,
so its pages lie on the earth near a torn-out stump,

13

the paper shrivelling into rain.

And the man who logged the Ridge
is finished with it, although he and the rest of us
constantly traverse its lowest levels
where the lane winds between our houses
and fields
toward the highway. Yet the Ridge
is not finished with the Valley
—its shadow continues to slip down its creekbeds
every afternoon
darkening the land as far as the river
while the other side still receives the sun.
That shadow, once of a forest,
now is born from an absence, from money,
from eight weeks' work.
We live each day shadowed by the Ridge,
neighbours of the man who cut it down.

THE CREEKS OF RICHARDS CREEK

Down from Perry's Ridge
by culvert under the Back Road
and the Lower Road
the creeks called Richards Creek
braid toward the river

a creek of clear water
a creek of rocks carried
to make its bed
a creek of sand for sheets
smoothing its way
a creek of chill air
flowing as the water's shadow
a creek of the sound
liquid coursing over stone
Also, a dark concrete water box
with buried pipes that fan out
to nearby houses
—a rigid creek
of human life

And the seventh creek
under thimbleberries
red-osier dogwood
ferns
a creek
secret, mysterious
protégé
of time

CABIN NEWS

Within the old wood cabin
is a world
pleasantly chill on sunny days
and now, with its stove disconnected,
cool also under rain.
Yet for decades, this interior was full of heat and steam
—a bathhouse or sauna:
many of the logs that support the ceiling
show burn-marks along their lengths.

                               At present
on the single room's walls
shelves hold stacks of books: the tumult of a society
with its fevered imagination
neatly packaged and still
unless you open one of these paper containers.
And every hour you don't
this place brings you cabin news:
the sound of Cadden Creek across the road
boisterous after a storm, a squirrel
chittering in the cedar at dawn,
wind pulling at the north window's plastic.

Herein is solitude, reflection:
a bed, table, cold water,
an elderly refrigerator mumbling
that even in this valley
ringed by mountains whose high ridges
are streaked with snow into early June
you cannot escape the mechanical constructions
distant men and women make.

But to live here for weeks
is to acquire secrets:
the texture of this cabin's changing light, its silences,
where its moths fly to rest.
The dwelling's shingled logs enclose a space you learn

the way a cow understands a field
better than its owner:
how certain branches hanging over a fence
provide shelter from a downpour, what portion of land
turns best to the sun at noon,
which slope offers refuge from the breeze
in a different time.

                    Nor does the cabin lack
a sense of humour. Electricity strung this far
must be carefully allocated
between lamps, hotplate, coffee pot and heater.
Guess wrong
or become inattentive
and a fuse trips the structure into dark and cold.
In the seconds after, you know the cabin
is mischievously teaching
what it imparts more solemnly
each ordinary moment of its presence:
"Be watchful
and respectful. Such conduct is
the path to joy."

                    Hills, B.C.

COUNTRY SOLITUDE

"Living alone out here—
how's your mental health?"
a visiting friend inquired over coffee
with a grin. "Started talking to yourself
yet?"
            Those are good questions,
I replied thoughtfully.
Just a minute and I'll check.
My friend's glance was quizzical
yet in fact I had been meaning to do
a little self-evaluation.
Listen up, everybody,
I announced. *You know the issue.*
Are we in the pink of emotional fitness
or what? A few voices
began to speak at once
and I observed my friend staring at me,
his mouth slightly open.
One at a time, one at a time,
I admonished. But the results I was getting
were mixed.
Okay, let's take a straw poll,
I decreed. The eyes of my friend
were flicking anxiously between me
and the door. *Quick,* I continued,
Those who think we're functioning well
put up your hands. Right.
Now, all who believe we might
have gone a bit off the rails
lift your hands.
My friend had risen from his chair.
I did a rapid addition.
Some of you aren't voting,
I noted sternly. *Let's try it again.*
My friend was fumbling at his jacket,
his lips pursed
as if silently whistling.

Yet the outcome of the vote was clear.
You don't have to worry about me
spending this time by myself,
I said in the direction of my friend's back
while he struggled with the doorknob.
We're doing fine.

COUNTRY PLEASURES

When I wake in the morning
I can tell by the frost on my beard
and the blanket
that both the electricity and the fire are out again.
I stagger into the washroom
but nothing comes from the taps
except a macabre rattle and gasp:
water line must have frozen solid
just like this time last year.
I'm about to descend to the basement
to see if I can rekindle the furnace at least
when the noise of an unusual commotion distracts me.
At first I think a bird or two
has fallen down the chimney once more
or perhaps the colony of wasps
who have settled in my outer walls
have decided to swarm. Yet when I follow the sound
to its source
I see to my horror a wounded deer chased by some dogs
has chosen my porch to die on.
I yank open the door and the dogs run away
but the deer, its sides heaving,
is pretty badly chewed up.
My rifle is of course at Norm's, the gunsmith,
for repairs
and those of my neighbours who aren't militant vegetarians
are on the other side than me of a bitter dispute
over a proposed clearcut of half the community watershed.
I reach for the phone,
meaning to inform the government Fish and Wildlife Branch
about the deer,
but find the two-year-old with whom I share my party line
has already begun his daily self-discovery
of telecommunication skills.
After some minutes of alternately wheedling
and commanding
her or him or it

to hang up the goddam phone so I can call for help
I discard this idea
and attempt to remember where I put the car keys.
I step onto my deck
walking around the apparently-comatose deer
who nevertheless opens its eyes as I pass
giving forth a piteous groan.
The car, only fifteen or twenty tries later, surges into life
and after checking both directions down the not-yet-plowed road
I head out toward the highway
and town.

COUNTRY INCOMPLETE

Nothing is ever finished
in the country:
house after house where siding
goes only part way up the walls
while around the dwelling are objects
once intended to be repaired or altered:
a pickup with its engine
on blocks beside it,
a hole in the ground that some Spring years ago
was to be a swimming pool,
an empty shed designed as a workshop
but never roofed: warped plywood covering half of it
and wire netting the rest
from months it served as a chicken coop.

Indoors, the situation
is identical: a sink not quite hooked up
so if you want to wash yourself
you fill a basin in the tub.
Or, a main floor with recognizable areas:
a corner with dishwasher and stove,
a spot where the couch, rug, stereo are grouped.
All that's absent
—and has been for as long as anyone can remember
—is the studding and sheetrock
to create rooms
(actually, studs *are* in place around the toilet,
with old blankets nailed across them
to serve as combination privacy screens and door).
These inconveniences, meant to be temporary,
soon get considered merely
arrangements—exactly as in other houses
someone did hang ceiling tiles
or has installed the linoleum.

From a distance, men and women in the country
seem to regard time as infinite:
what isn't completed today
won't get done tomorrow either.
Partly the problem is
that whoever wants to resume work on a project
must obtain a certain size of clamp
or a particular electrical connector
in town. These missing components
are on a list somewhere
perhaps lost under a car seat
or in the space behind the refrigerator.

> To adults, years when cupboard doors aren't hung
> or the back steps built
> are only an interval
> in a busy life. One day, however,
> a son or daughter is through with school
> and leaves home, and the parents realize
> their offspring's entire childhood
> was spent on a construction site.

Yet if an excuse is needed
for all this delay
any of us in the country have only to gaze
out the front window (still tacked in place,
waiting to be properly insulated).
The mountains, river, even the garden
are never finished either:
erosion, the seasons
go on shaping the natural world
into a series of transitional forms.
In the city, there is an illusion of closure:
in whole districts a majority of houses

appear to have every board
neatly in place, painted, with lawns
perfectly clipped and edged.
Yet in a city, too, rain and wind
are always present
and, inside, time
is taking the bloom off the fanciest wallpaper.
Underneath the metropolis, creeks
that once drained this region
and are now constricted into pipes
surface after a storm
in the middle of an avenue
or the basement of a highrise.
Like rural people, water and weather and time
are never satisfied
but constantly start to transform the environment,
then become distracted
and initiate an additional project
they believe will also help them feel at home.

Such tentativeness, though, is more noticeable
in the country. Thus maybe poems
about nature, and especially about the lives
along back roads and gravel lanes,
shouldn't be brought to a
resounding conclusion
but,
instead...

Kootenay Anthem

A blue sky over these mountains
this June, and I hear rising toward it
music: the bass theme
of the valleys' roads, barns, houses,
and the lines of utility poles'
quick staccato, lighter airs of the wires' curve
and climb, and of the logging tracks
threading far up the ridges

But subsuming each of these melodies
is a green anthem of the sea of trees
flooding these ranges: each fir or spruce
an intricately-fashioned cathedral
and the slopes crowded with
cathedrals—alder and birch,
cedar and larch
Hillsides
of cathedrals, each filled
with its own choral harmony
merging and counterpointing
within, and with all other musics
so every song uttered on this continent
by the tribes, the pioneers, ourselves
and each song that is to be
is lifted simultaneously from these peaks
and valleys, the notes
pulsing into one colossal, variegated
tune of green

In the sunshine, halfway up a mountain
named three times, but a mountain
without a name, a
tree
stands
and sings

ASSURANCE OF RIVERS

I

On Perry's Ridge, Jerome Creek
overflows its waterbox
in June, refinding its old descent
towards the River,
transmitting the steady irregular pulse
of liquid pushing over stone

But once under the Valley road
by culvert, the water
begins to lose its
instinctive purpose
as a meadow
clutches at it, cajoles it, flatters it
The stream
slows and becomes distracted
splits and wanders away
then rejoins itself
but soon twins again
and curves in odd directions
always less itself
when it reforms, until
the primal motion stops:
a puddle
on boggy ground
still hundreds of metres
from the River
which continues to quickly, steadily pass,
uttering no comment
on this creek's failure
to thrive

II

Evans Creek, in Spring
carries part of the snowpack down
from the crests
of the Valhalla Ranges
Each tributary
—Beatrice Creek
and others—
brings molten ice
white from the high country,
from mountain-ringed
alpine lakes,
descending
the clefts and gullies
of the ridges,
calling in
more melt and also
the June rains
until
the creek bloats,
smashes down the last rockfalls
in a hoarse continual shout
of power
and bulls into the Lake

from which the River
departs to the south
bearing this creek's enormity of
fluid
as one insignificant component
of its volume
as it spreads below the Lake
over the low benches and fields
along its banks,
yet everywhere propelling itself swiftly:

the River's aim this season,
as throughout the year,
to empty, empty the mountains
of their icy water
—a task equivalent to
draining
the sea

HEADLANDS

> *Each day is a journey, and the*
> *journey itself home.*
>
> —Basho

My car accelerates over a crest
and begins to drop
the road weaving tightly
along the contours of this hillside
In the distance
a vista of lake
with mountain after mountain on the other side
Our planet has swung around the sun
more than twenty times since I began
to travel these highways alone
Already in this frantically short lifetime
the rivers of this land have worn themselves
passages through my flesh, two crows
bother an eagle above a tall fir
in a cleared space in my mind, promontories
jut toward the bay or inlet
in the form my organs take
that themselves shape my outer skin
I descend this slope
while the tires follow the easy curves of the asphalt
turn and turn
and I find these hollows and swellings
within myself
When I rise from the lakeshore
ascending over a ridge again
I will lift
in my spirit, in the road's climb
and fall toward
grace, the long route: home

HEART MOUNTAIN

GETTING THE NEWS

At her words, the small boy inside me
is shoved face forward
trips, hits gravel
and begins to slide
Palms and knees tear open
the flesh peels back
like flames shrivelling paper
Grains of rock embed themselves
in the expanding cuts
so when I coast to a stop
in a blur of pain
and stand shakily erect
I attempt only once to brush clear
skinned flesh:
my blunt hands
force gravel further into my wounds
Alone on the road
my hurts filming over with blood
I swallow air
ready to howl my agony
swallow air
air

WHEN THE HEART HAS LOST WHAT IT DESIRED

it stops still:
a horse alone in a field
in a heavy downpour
stunned by the tremendous pull
of the planet its hooves touch
and the weight of the rain.
At the road's edge
autumn has choked the green ferns
turning them sere
and brown. Behind a house and barn
golden-yellow alder and larch
mottle the abrupt slope
of mountainside.
The horse
stands under a nearly leafless tree
skin and hair soaked
by the continually falling water.
The horse remembers
in summer this tree was a roof:
that is why it remains here
motionless
letting the rain descend.
The horse could choose
anywhere in the chill field
to exist
and it would be just as sodden.
The horse does not know
if it will ever be dry
and comfortable
or if this weather has settled in
for the season
or is permanent.
The horse can conceive
only this response:

immobility
and a wish to shame the tree
for having abandoned
its use as shelter
—a stoic act
in the face of raging anxiety.

THE NAIL

When love
one of a couple wants greatly
is denied
a certain nerve leading into the heart
begins to stiffen.
A span of the nerve about four fingers long
almost buried within the organ
then detaches from the rest.
This extent of nerve
continues hardening
until it is
a nail jabbed in the heart.

The end of the nerve at the deepest point
emits a sharp pain
with each regular contraction.
Flesh and muscle along the length of the nail
become tender and inflamed.
Now the nail must be removed.
As with a spike clenched by wood,
the nail must be pried loose,
creaking, its slow movement at first
agony against the raw edges
of its passage.

And when the nail finally is clear of the body
there is danger the opening left behind
will turn septic, obsessive.
How to heal this wound
the healthiest way
is the subject of various studies and tracts.
Where the nail was
lies empty, vulnerable,
hurtful to the touch
and many kinds of motion.

HEART WATER

And the heart, from time to time
is a fish
grown too large
for its fleshy aquarium.
It thrashes madly
against the walls
then collapses for minutes
scarcely moving a fin.
This heart-fish
is obsessed
with the fixation
of all imperiled creatures
to repeat
to repeat
what has not yet saved them:
a dog fallen into the water of
a boathouse
scrabbling desperately to
climb the slippery logs
onto the walkway
while behind his drawn-out
frantic explosion of foam
an open door allows
an easy swim around to the beach.
This fish, too
cannot reason
in its distress.
So certain chords of music
a couple of names
some blocks of specific avenues
and one or two moments
in the calendar

prod the heart
to rotate hysterically
in its cage.
Such exertions
plus sweat from the elastic walls
that confine the heart
transform the fluid here
first to salt water
then to salt.

The Heart Is Also A Meadow

The heart is also
a mountain meadow
a tangle thigh-deep of
hay, ferns
purple thistle
Indian paintbrush
the intense minuscule blue
of forget-me-not
tall angelica along a creekbed
and white-and-brown daisies
scattered everyplace
but especially where years ago
a dirt road curved through

Much could be hidden
in this foliage:
a grouse nest
with five eggs
a sudden charge by the grouse herself
or a bear
that rises out of grass
a few metres away
as if a troop of mounted warriors from another age
lifted up on their horses
weapons and tackle jangling
in the still air

Deer
thread across the meadow
by moonlight

while from a nest aloft
in the brain-stem tree
five ravens

watch

and cry out

Near one edge of this clearing
a cabin
of planks and steeply angled tin roof
stands
None of the ordinary litter
of human habitation
surrounds it
There is only the grass
and then abruptly
this dwelling
It could be the home
of a witch
or hermit—
the door is sealed
with a rusty padlock
Yet the structure
is in good repair
its windows shuttered
from within
awaiting the return of
whatever once
lived here

THE TIDES OF THE HEART

I

The heart
contains a tiny sea.
In the world outside, the salty ocean
is hauled two ways by the moon.
But within, besides this ebb and flood
—systole, diastole—
rage can sweep across
the heart's waters:
a minuscule Spring storm
that howls and pounds against the coast,
increasing in fury until some influence or
draw
shifts the liquid's depth and direction
and begins to restore the small globe
to a tranquil appearance.

          Or grief
or profound disappointment
may render the interior sea
motionless,
lowering its temperature until the waters thicken
and freeze.
Unlike the Earth's polar oceans
that circulate under the icecap,
the heart's fluid
becomes entirely chill and solid.
In the ghastly quiet,
the ice expands outward
against the fleshy walls that hold it.
The body experiences first soreness,
then torment.

          Such suffering
can trigger panic: perhaps the heart
will be unable to confine

the slow, inexorable swelling of ice
and may rupture
and die.
Fear
tightens the muscles of the organ's walls
which increases the anguish.

Yet the heart
usually survives.
Though it takes months
or years, some external attraction
causes a change in the stresses
within the frozen sea.
A slight trickle
begins.
This reduces the cold a little
and starts to unlock more liquid
from its icy state

until one evening
the heart again
flows easily between its ordinary shores.

II

But what moon
tugs the heart's salt fluid,
causes these tides
and others:
the aromatic currents
of affection, the tropical surges of
carnality, choppy surface
of anxiousness, the slack water
of contentment? Is it the brain
looming above
that alters this miniature ocean?

Or, since so many different tides
transform the organ
is there more than one
moon?
Each of the senses, possibly?
Or is the heart
self-motivated,
functioning according to
some hidden source
at its liquid core:
as a black hole
invisible at a galaxy's centre
creates interstellar tides
of gravitational pull and
fluctuations
—affecting objects inconceivable distances away
across space
and time?

One Friday, at the beginning of the weekly meeting
Heart announced:
"You can take my item
off the agenda."
"I don't believe it,"
Liver said. "It's been the main subject we've discussed
for months."
"I don't seem to need
to talk about it any more," Heart said.
"Are you sure?"
Brain inquired
from the chair. "What happened is a serious concern
affecting us all. It may be premature to..."
"You heard him, you heard him,"
Lower Bowel interrupted.
"At *last* we can consider something else.
Please don't try to change his mind."
"Yeah, some of us were mentioning
before the rest of you showed up
how sick we are of this topic," Lungs said.
"Add you're only speaking medaphorically,"
Nasal Passages sniffed.
"I god saddled with the old
psychosomatic heavy."
"That was by majority vote,"
Brain said. "Back said he was tired
of carrying the weight..."
"No pun intended," a lymph node chimed in.
"...And the others agreed," Brain continued firmly.
"This is a collective, not a dictatorship.
If any of you don't like the way I chair these gatherings
you can ask for a recall."
"Don't we want to hear *why*
Heart feels finished with this problem?" Stomach said.
There was instant quiet
as all eyes rotated toward Heart.
"Really, I've taken up too much of your time," Heart said.

"That's for sure,"
Lower Bowel said loudly.
"I know I've been obsessive about it,"
Heart resumed. "I just feel now I have a better handle
on dealing with it. Of course,"
Heart went on quickly, "that's due in large part
to the help I've received here. I'm very grateful."
"Don't let these negative folks influence you,"
Brain said. "I want to remind everybody
that when our friend Heart is on top of things
we're all purring and happy.
When he's down the least we can do
is lend a sympathetic ear."
"We've lent till we're broke ourselves,"
a voice along the table muttered.
"Say again?" Brain asked. Then, after a moment:
"If Heart is on the road to recovery,
that's good news. We should be pleased."
A silence. Brain cleared his throat.
"Okay. Any new items for the meeting?
I mean *external* issues, not more bickering among ourselves."
"Well," Spleen said,
"there's one matter
that's started to really bug me..."

MODIFICATIONS TO THE HEART

In a child, the heart is plump
but strong with the tenseness
of young limbs.
Occasionally, though, an event
will tear open the covering of the organ
like a knee scraped bloody in a spill from a bicycle.
The wound is painful for days,
then heals completely.

Yet insecurities
or a hideous incident or situation
involving the boy or girl
can grip the heart
and twist it
to a barely recognizable shape.
Thus the modification of the heart
may commence early—the organ might or might not
ever recover its whole function.

And for each person there awaits a first
betrayal or loss
usually experienced in adolescence
that permanently marks the heart,
even if the only evidence years later
is a slight nick or scar.
Thereafter, the blows begin to strike
with increasing rapidity
in the normal course of adult love
and rejection.
Mostly these assaults
result in bruises and other surface discolouration
that disappear in time
but underlying tissue also can be injured.
The latter damage, as with some childhood hurt
that weakened subsurface muscle and fibres,
might be undetected for years
until a portion of the heart one Thursday after a meal
collapses.

And from time to time, a wound is inflicted so deeply
—either in a single moment
with a sharp blow like a knife's
or in an jagged tear
ripped slowly apart during weeks or months
of excruciating pain—
that medical intervention is required.
This can take the form of stitches
or a metal or plastic plate must be implanted
to hold the heart together.
Or, tissue from the brain
or lungs or stomach
must be grafted across the cut.

More ordinary disappointments,
confrontations
and setbacks
also affect the heart:
the thousands of daily jabs
of electrical or adrenalin shock
leave areas of each atrium and ventricle
pockmarked or excessively spongy,
tenderer than usual
or abnormally thickened and coarse.

Such changes to the heart are clearly evident
by a person's forties.
It is common for a man or woman in that decade
to remove the heart
and examine it, noting the differences
from when he or she was younger
and attempting to account for the obvious devastation.
The battered heart sits on a cloth
in front of them, its convoluted surface a morass
of healed and half-healed
notches, slits
and contusions.
Sections of it may have gone dead

45

from stress or trauma,
other parts are engorged with blood
because of too-active capillaries.
Yet as the owner of the heart watches,
the organ effortlessly
contracts and
expands, apparently capable of absorbing
more
adverse treatment—
of continuing to sustain
a human life.

THE HOUSĖD HEART

This time, after six months of searching
I located a wide meadow
not far from a road
and stream. There were some negotiations
and I assumed
the spot. I began to build
in a familiar, happy frenzy
—out at the site each morning
already hammering when the sun
crested the eastern ridge. I sang
through my days, above the shrill roar
of the saw, or in the mountain silence
between tasks, or with the remnants of my breath
as I hauled boards
to where they were next needed.
Old tunes came back to me:
folk ballads and raucous
or sentimental melodies
of childhood.

And the new house
sparkled
—its clean lines
as perfect as I could construct them;
the new windows gleamed
as the sunset struck
the dwelling's freshly painted siding.

Until a month
after I began
a full moon pushed up from among the firs
at the top of the valley.
As her rays
touched the foundation
the cement started to bubble
then sag. When her beams
brushed against the new walls

the wood cried aloud in pain
and buckled; the windows
melted. I knew none of this
until the next morning
when I jumped out of the truck
before what my eyes from a distance
could not believe.
Everything I had laboured on
was decayed.
The roof and sides
were black, weathered timber
and the building wrenched open
where the centre of the structure
had collapsed.
A shambles of planks and joists and rafters
splintered around the edges of the great hole
that nearly severed
the house.
And the boards visible within
were stained dark
from years of rain.

Cargo

Sure, I Was Paid Well

but the money felt
like a thick stack of bills
had been folded once and crammed in my open mouth

so what I wanted to say
was blocked, or at the very least garbled
by the wad of dollars

                          and my jaws ached
with the strain of being held apart
by the cash. Though I tried to dress well

I wasn't sure if people on the street
mocked me behind my back
for being so funny-looking

with a mouth stuffed with currency.
Or maybe they didn't see me at all
but only saw the clump of bills

that pressed down on my tongue.
When I sought out others paid as much as me
I found myself calculating how thick

their gag of dollars was
compared to mine. In any case
it was difficult to talk about the experience we had in common

since their words were hard to distinguish
through the money. And I confess
I was afraid to stick my fingers in behind

and lever the currency out; I was fearful of
what was dammed up
behind that cash,

of what the absence of those dollars
would release. And I was anxious
that the wad of money

would turn out to be an illusion:
a few genuine bills on the outside of the roll
and the rest only paper,

paper.

DID I MISS ANYTHING?

Question frequently asked by
students after missing a class

Nothing. When we realized you weren't here
we sat with our hands folded on our desks
in silence, for the full two hours

       Everything. I gave an exam worth
       40 per cent of the grade for this term
       and assigned some reading due today
       on which I'm about to hand out a quiz
       worth 50 per cent

Nothing. None of the content of this course
has value or meaning
Take as many days off as you like:
any activities we undertake as a class
I assure you will not matter either to you or me
and are without purpose

       Everything. A few minutes after we began last time
       a shaft of light descended and an angel
       or other heavenly being appeared
       and revealed to us what each woman or man must do
       to attain divine wisdom in this life and
       the hereafter
       This is the last time the class will meet
       before we disperse to bring this good news to all people
           on earth

Nothing. When you are not present
how could something significant occur?

       Everything. Contained in this classroom
       is a microcosm of human existence

assembled for you to query and examine and ponder
This is not the only place such an opportunity has been
    gathered

but it was one place

And you weren't here

CORRECTING 120 ESSAYS ON POETRY

My task is dry
as brittle paper
the red pencil
scratching scratching
—sand
caught between metal parts
forced to slide
open/shut

Sometimes what they have created
is strangely
beautiful:
a wooden sculpture
almost spherical
half the size
of a basketball
I run my palms and fingers
around and around it
notice a rough part
write: *awkward; could be smoother*
at this spot
Later they read my comment
Their eyes say
I know that

Or
what they hand in
is shaped in a rush
or crude
grotesque
because they were absent
or inattentive
when the directions were given
they did not know
were thinking of other problems, joys
I examine each of these constructs
just as gravely as the others

rotating them before me
on the desk
Such creations seem
a rejected version
a piece
left with the shavings and wood chips
under a workbench
after a false start
or dropped by mistake
My hands travel
across the surface
find a deep furrow
gouged
I write *you have a furrow*
here
But when the makers
hold again what they devised
they do not read
any words: their eyes
seek the letter
or number I attach
to this broken thing
When they read that
they nod
toss the malformed object
away

COLLEAGUE

Even at a meeting
with other faculty
when she turns to
the chalkboard
she scratches at it
with exact angry strokes
slashing the hard
lines of the letters of words
down on the vertical surface
incising
as into stone
both
what she wants to write
what she cannot say

Hurdlers

After they have chosen to pay
the considerable fee to race
and spent more to purchase personal equipment
and put time aside to prepare themselves

I get hired.
My job is to introduce them to a series of actions
I believe will result in an advantage
for them, an improvement
in the results they can
accomplish. For months
I take them through these steps,
these practices.

But periodically
they must assemble for a meet.
I conduct them to the place,
show them the hurdles ahead
in their lanes,
remind them of successes they have already
achieved

and at the signal
they are away.
Yet despite everything we have considered together,
always a few of them
dash to the first of the small gates
and stop.
No, no, they announce loudly
you don't get me
to jump one of those.
"Why not?" I pant anxiously
having dashed over
to see what could be wrong.
Never mind, they say,
folding their arms
as if they had previously rehearsed

what they are about to utter:
No way am I going over that.
No way.
The other men and women who started beside them
are plunging and rising in the distance.

I begin to babble
about how much they have invested
to date in these procedures;
I offer deals, praise,
threats, reason.
But these balkers stand
unshakeable,
confident of this decision
their knowledge has led them to,
possessed of a great truth.

I stare at them
out of my uncertain eyes
—even the sounds of the others
having vanished ahead;

they are so sure
of their refusal
facing them is like looking into the sun.

First-Year English Final

These seem papers
singed by fire
—documents left scattered
in a hectic retreat of
battalion headquarters
or the abandoned records
of an overthrown regime

Fear and pain
shimmer over the disorganized pages
hover above the words scratched along the slots
lined onto the white surface

And rage
flares in the ink
deposited frantically here
It is anger that matches my own
knuckle to knuckle
as I read the words
as my red pen
descends toward its victims
toward what is written
Once more
I have failed
to convince, to inform
to teach

  So I hold their fury
  stacks of it
  sheets of it
  and press down on theirs
  with my own

    How did literature
    become so filled
    with hate?

Document your sources correctly
the red nib admonishes
You must provide examples
to show *what you mean*

The blue paragraphs
howl
WE DID NOT ASK TO DO THIS

No one is listening

FACING IT

A bad morning at my house:
refrigerator light burns out,
a leak in a basement water pipe.
I trip on a throw rug
I've walked over flawlessly
thirty thousand times.

Pushed to my limit
I find myself in the living room
in a fighter's crouch, fists lifted and clenched,
haranguing the furniture:
"Okay, okay, who's next?
Who else intends to screw up?
C'mon, step forward.
Let's get it over with."
The sofa and chairs remain silent,
cowed, abashed.
I continue to stare them down.
"I'm ready," I snarl.
"If you're going to act up,
do it now, eyeball to eyeball,
man to man."
The lamps and rug say nothing,
gaze at the floor.
"All right, then," I declare
looking meaningfully at each one.
"We'll have no more fooling around."
I strut out of the room,
tension draining from my body.

The day looks better already.

THE ICEBERG, THE SHADOW

A line of cars
speeds down the freeway.
Alongside this road, woodlots alternate with light industry.
A truck dealership,
discount furniture enterprises,
approach and then fall behind.
And underneath each vehicle
regardless of lane
or rate of motion
coasts
a Shadow.

Plato was wrong
about shadows.
These are not the darkened outline
the Ideal casts
into the cave of this world.

The Shadow every object throws
is the visible memoir
of the human lives
interwoven with the presence of this thing
on the earth:
the woman, the man
who gathered the materials
from which the object is formed,
who designed,
assembled,
tested, shipped,
stocked, sold.
How doing this work
felt,
the way each task
structured, directed,
harmed or enhanced

the days and nights of the individual
who performed it.

All such actions,
concepts,
existences,
appear now as a blackness
hurtling down pavement
under drivetrains, fuel tanks, muffler piping
that accelerate and switch lanes,
or suddenly brake
before returning to a constant pace again.

Even the asphalt
projects *its* Shadow
on the soil below
or on air and water
where the highway lifts over a river.

Yet what we observe as Shadow
is as ice
in salt water: beneath these cars
is shown
one tenth
of what their being in this world involves:
how these men and women
came to do this job,
the origin of the work itself,
why the tasks
are organized as they are,
the history of fire, tools,
wages, the shortcuts and substitutions
necessary to keep production numbers
at a level acceptable
to someone farther up the hierarchy
—these aspects among others
are pulled through the earth,

connected to what passes above
but unseen.

My hope is for a time
when that which is hidden
will be openly revealed,
considered,
changed for our benefit.
When this process commences,
we will first observe the Shadow under each object
lengthen.
Then, imperceptibly at first,
the Shadow will grow lighter, become translucent
and finally
dissolve
precisely as an iceberg
that reaches warmer waters
returns
the full cargo of itself
to the source
of all.

TIDES

As the sea incessantly
reoccupies the border
it shares with land
so when I am without funds
for a time, then suddenly employed
I begin
to pay off debts
until there is a drop
for savings
and another, that slowly merge
into a puddle
then a pool, creeping sideways
to touch other funds
at hand, until I am completely awash
with money, the tide
is in

      But large purchases
I have postponed
or the steady daily expenditures
once the job has ended
start to drain
what has taken so long to gather
The sea of cash
ebbs remorselessly
uncovering
a white beach
empty
in my passbook
—a space
like a gleaming new coin
no longer mine

How I Became A Planet

THE GIFT

Let me explain how it happened,
friends. Because I was afraid
you wouldn't like me if I didn't,
I gave all you appeared to ask for
and then some. In the end
I found a limit
to what I had to dispense:
every bit of
me
was gone.

            Don't blame yourselves.
I needed to hand you this much
to be happy. I didn't comprehend
your first choice
wasn't my gifts; you would rather have had
more of who I was
and less of what I was able to provide.

Yes, I had warnings. After a day of philanthropy
I would return home exhausted
and there, at one basis of my life,
I had no strength to bestow
or enjoy. Of course the worse this got
the more frantically I donated
all I could elsewhere.

I would wake in the dark and smell smoke
along my arms and legs.
Inside my flesh
my skeleton was smouldering.
I would shake with terror:
everything that might have put out this fire
I had given away.

So I ran
to the mountains, alone

where there would be no person
to whom I could provide any thing.
My intent is to find out
if what I dispensed from
is like a water box on a water line
that slowly fills again
if drained dry.

This is the reason I crave
the return of those parts of myself
you hold—although I never intended
that which I granted you
to be accounted for, later.

If, through your good graces
or natural processes, I am restored,
I want an end to the fears
that led me to act as I did.
I want to understand
true generosity
and its boundaries.

And if I am not replenished
I need to learn how best to function
this empty, this solitary,
this free.

LAUNCHING

I tugged the slipknot
on the last rope to a mooring ring
and lifted off
At first I rose slowly
but soon gazed down from a considerable height
at the upturned faces drifting astern
As I floated
I was wrapped in a quiet
so total the focus of my hearing
became the slight sound of a clock
on the cabin wall
and the little battery-powered refrigerator
a creak in the floorboards as I walk

When the ground had receded to a stable distance
I knew I had reached my traveling altitude
and turned from the windows
to various tasks and chores
At first, life aloft was an adventure
—cooking, washing at the small sink
lying in the strange bed at night
—each elemental aspect of existence
fresh again, as when I was a child
Even after a week
when I was more used to the experience
I still got up in the night and wandered
through the gondola's rooms
peering far below at
the slowly shifting lights
Savoring such moments, alone in the dark
I am suffused with a joy
I have not felt for years
—as though I have attained
some accomplishment rich in rewards and satisfactions
the way birthdays or Christmases were
long ago

Nor am I isolated here: the gondola
contains an air-to-ground telephone
But the rare calls, one every two or three days
are mostly routine position checks, weather reports
In the first week after takeoff
there was a flurry of contacts from friends
but this soon ended
Their absence upset me
This is what being dead must feel like
I thought
Everyone you know continues with their lives
in which you are now reduced
to an occasional flicker of memory
or less
But then I saw from a porthole
the sun shining from a sheet of blue water
the light broken into dazzling particles
by the tiny waves
This is what it is to be
alive, I decided
My former hours chained to my need for people
were more death than this
As if sensing my change in perception
friends began to phone again
wanting now to express their anger
"How dare you just float away?
You always were selfish!"
"Don't you care?" Their thin voices
carry across kilometres of air
messages from another life
from people I never knew well
or, though I often stood beside them
I could not see

"And where are you *going*?" one asks
and I have no reply
Perhaps I am waiting to learn this
myself

or maybe circumstances that have nothing to do with me
will influence my destination
Yet the longer I am airborne
the more control
I seem to have over the voyage
This might be a delusion
spawned from too many days of solitude
Or, since we live in a random universe
what motion isn't a drift
unanchored, across the expanse we name time

In silence
I am soaring across the Earth
as the Earth in turn
traverses space
I believe I am sailing
into myself
or that the voyage
is myself
But this act could be
only travel: cloud mountains
sky water
fiery sun
moon air

NICE GUY

I decided, after a time,
my activities must be approved
by those nearest me
so they will like who I am
and—more important—won't be angry
at me.
Ever since I saw a person's rage
as a hammer smashed through glass,
as my self
obliterated,
anger became an environmental hazard.
I began to diligently inquire:
Is it okay with you
if I do this?
"What a thoughtful guy,"
people say at first, but friends
after hearing too often
my relentless query:
Is it all right if I…?
Is it okay?
eventually lash out:
"Stop!"
Such rejection
—being the exact response
my behaviour was designed to prevent—
generates a certain amount of negative emotion
in me: *How can they feel this*
when my question was for their *benefit?*

> And, strangely, my fear of disapproval
> has not kept me from volunteering
> in the struggle over social issues.
> On the line,
> I had a brother collapse beside me
> with a night stick slammed into his gut,
> stood up with a sister
> shouting toward a building

guarded by helmets and guns,
carried more than my share of cardboard signs,
attended twenty thousand meetings.

But driving a carfull
to such gatherings
my voice continues to repeat:
Do you mind
if I park here? If I stop for gas
after the rally?

    In fact, what I desire
    to happen close around me
    I somehow arrange
    despite my solicitous questioning.
    At home, too,
    I ask and ask
    until it's clear I'm present to fulfil
    whatever the woman I'm with requires
    —rescue, encouragement and
    to be provided for. Yet my own wishes
    and needs
    are busy in the shadows
    and my actions there
    hurt everything that occurs in the light.

One curious effect
of my aim not to cause any trouble
—while surreptitiously trying to achieve
all I feel I'm due—
has been a concern to keep my possessions
properly ordered and maintained:
a house with clean floors,
papers and clothes
neatly put away,
any of the leaks, cracks or clutter
that materialize where human beings spend their hours

fixed at once, or abolished.
My goal seems to be to pass through life
having made no visible ripple,
to hear somebody pronounce:
"After years
your car still looks new."
When in other people's homes, also,
my goal is to exist invisibly;
I dream of my death in hospital
and a nurse saying later:
"Hard to believe
someone was dying in that room just an hour ago.
Look how tidy
he left everything. It's like
he was never here."

       Only with words
       do I want to make a personal impact.
       Ah, but few objects
       are more insubstantial than words
       spoken, vibrating in the ear
       and then vanishing as completely
       as English itself will one day.
       How unobtrusive.
       Or, better: words that are read silently,
       not disturbing even the molecules of the air.
       Only a few electrical connections
       are noiselessly made in a brain
       and forgotten, or if remembered
       that brain will exist only a limited time
       before whisking what it has stored
       into the clean perpetual dark.

Could anything be less bothersome?
Surely such behaviour
wouldn't be opposed?

If you disagree, though,
I hope you don't mind
me mentioning all this.

THICKET

As I press forward, a knotted mass of projections
extends from my body
—short wires that bristle, much longer ones with
frayed ends dragging on the ground
aerials that jut at odd angles
from arms, shoulder, torso
metal coils rising and drooping
a snarl of ropes and cable
coating a thigh or elbow

Around me, other men and women
equally encumbered
are proceeding
The extensions of a few of them
tangle tightly with mine: family, friends
As we move, an antenna
is snapped off, other connections
are broken, and different bits of wire
originating from our separate selves
twist around each other in a new way

But every person
does not travel at an identical pace
or in the same direction
So I am overtaken
or overtake
this human being or that
We become linked or jammed together
and either pull abruptly apart
or struggle on alongside each other
for a distance, tugging at or
relaxing what has bound us
or even interacting in a kind of harmony
for a time

Occasionally someone cuts in front
or confronts me
and I am blocked
Both of us jerk angrily
at our new bonds
If our jostling and shoving
become too frenzied
projections are ripped completely out of
their fleshy sockets
in a blaze of pain
When one of us is significantly stronger
the other can be dragged a short distance
from his or her intended path
But since each of us is firmly joined
to other strangers, friends, relatives
neither of us can haul the other
entirely in our own direction of travel
We try to lunge toward freedom
ignoring the hurt of torn-away parts of ourselves
or stop and work to separate
the unwanted links between us

Since such events reoccur continually
to each of those tied closest to us
everyone's progress is slow
Yet in this manner we journey
conscious or unconscious of the thicket
of spines and cords
wrapped around us
gathering all we encounter
into a tangled whole

Exploring Tom Wayman

I

When it became vital to me
to stop relying on luck
and intense activity
to attain happiness,
when I needed to examine my failures with people
and with myself,
I looked for the first time at where I stood.
I saw my feet were on a path
closed by rockslides.
I chipped samples from the stones that impeded me,
wanting to better comprehend them,
raised portions of them glittering to the light
and talked about them cheerfully for weeks.

But none assayed out
as successfully as I expected.
I perceived that what I thought were nuggets
were only hardened portions of cord or rope
lying on the surface of
a large jumble of such cable.
I set myself the task to untangle,
with counsel, this gnarled mound
until it stretched in front of me
orderly, accessible,
safe.

As I attempted to unravel
the sections I had pried loose,
I imagined this undertaking
would be like dismantling an onion:
peeling layer after layer
to reveal the secrets of its centre.
Yet the more I probed,
painfully inserting marlinspike and crowbar
and applying weight,

I realized I had to chart and assess
not the gigantic clump of twisted wire
but what had extruded the pile:
a newly discovered planet.

Since then, I've learned this sphere
named after myself
has a molten core
around which are solidified overlays that reveal
vastly different geologic experiences.
These include the depositing of ancient sediments
that over eons
result in the emergence of stratified rock.
Also, shafts of volcanic ejecta
long ago forced their way out
to coat the surface
with their particular point of view.
This process created columns
of igneous material, seared and hard.
Within the variegated crust as well,
remain pockets of diverse temperatures and pressures,
and the sudden, or slow, shift
of immense blocks of stone
in slippages like earthquakes
or mountain building
or in the wandering of continental plates.
I understand that the knotted self I project to the world
is constantly shaped by
such historic and current transformations.
What I had regarded initially as significant discoveries
are only the outcrop of much bigger events
extending back, in some cases,
for incomprehensible generations.
Then, too, the weariness of erosion
and other weathering
continues to fracture and complicate
how I appear externally, no less a factor in who I am

than my varied composition within.

To know myself,
I am now aware,
means mastering a science
as precise and unsure
as geology: careful measurements
and wild guesses,
the testing and destruction of theories
in labs full of sterilized instruments
or on paper, aided by
mathematical printouts
and hours of study.
Research teams must be always
in the field, tirelessly gathering evidence
and labelling, packing and shipping samples
for later analysis.

II

As for me, I go out these days
with reports, graphs, statistics
in one hand, and in the other a hammer.
If my voice sounds strange to you
it is because it may be coming
from far down a pit I have dug,
or from following a vein of ore
in a mine tunnelled along a fissure of rock.
Even more difficult for me
than all this busyness
is to sit and observe
some minuscule gradual development
or to wait patiently for an assessment of data
to be completed by the months-behind
panel of consultants or resident staff.

And steadily the dimensions
of the questions I have posed
expand: how did I grow
this planet, why did I wait so many years
to begin exploring it,
will there be a beneficial outcome
of any discovery
—other than the proverb's claim
about knowledge being its own reward?
As information pours in from various sources
—some facts clarifying a difficulty,
other bits compounding
an already convoluted problem—
I at times believe the whole history of science
is unfolding at high speed in my head:
classical theorists, mystical proposals, cranks,
modest proponents of
world-shaking concepts,
exhibitionists waving the flimsiest of evidence
on which to erect elegant and appealing texts.
How much simpler it was for me
when I was only a person
and not a planet.
I remember, though, how my simplicity
led to considerable harm to myself and others
as innocence in any form
often does.
Yet whether the evolution of learning
and the ability to translate knowledge into
feeling
and appropriate action
have progressed to a level capable of
resolving any issue
is one *more* answer
I am seeking to find.

Return to the Heart

The sound of the river had not changed:
the glacial torrent cutting between
black rock piled on rock
scattered down this valley one season
when water poured over the mountain barrier.
I crouched to drink
in the midst of the icy spray
and the throbbing
of the river pushing among these stones.

Where the stream widens
to form an island of
alder and cottonwood
the water is fast, but not deep
and it is possible to cross
cautiously balancing from rock to rock.
Twenty-five years ago
I came alone once to this place
a boy near the edge of adulthood
carrying my heart.

           I recall
how for most of a morning
I built a structure of poles and stones.
I took a small bag from my pack
and mixed concrete at the pebbled edge of the island
then took my heart
and set it
at the centre of what I had constructed
and sealed it in
and turned away.

    I had decided I did not need
    whatever uses the organ served.
    For years after, I worked at my life.
    I had what I thought were good friends
    and lovers, walked in fire

and deep cold, laughed much and
felt sharp pain.

But in the cavity in my chest
where the heart was absent
a fluid unknown to medicine
began to collect. At the start the liquid seemed benign
a sort of protective secretion
but after more than two decades
the fluid
shifts
throwing me off balance
when I bend too abruptly toward or
back from another person. Also the liquid
has become acidic
searing the tissue that contains it.

When I described my symptoms
my doctors made notes
and referred me to other physicians.
At last, though, I remembered
my heart.

So I have returned to this wood
with a new pack on my shoulders
and with sledge hammer and shovel.
After the hike in from the old road
I located the island
more densely treed now.
I left my gear on the beach where I crossed
and began to search for
a small mound of cement.

For hours I dodged branches
forcing my way amid the alder trunks and bushes.
Sometimes I crawled across a likely spot
feeling with my hand through high grass

or scrabbling amid roots and stones.
At lunchtime, I found a clearing in the undergrowth
and retrieved my pack and equipment
and sat to eat
watching birds and a squirrel in the leaves above me
and the play of light
where the river leapt and fell back.
Near the finish of my meal
I reached to place the cup of my thermos
on a rocky outcrop
and was aware that under moss
this was my heart's grave.

My hands began to shake.
What would be left of my heart
after this long in the dark:
a crumble of dust, or
a desiccated leather bag
or could the organ be
somehow undamaged
by its stay within an airtight space
far from blood and breath?

I scrape off moss
baring grey concrete
and heft the sledge.
Each time the head falls
it bounces once
on the surface
and subsides. I lift my arms
over my right shoulder
and smash the sledge down.
In my ears
is the deafening ring
of steel on stone.

DARK MIRROR

How close, how sudden
the dark mirror
appears

A pain in my gut
swelling from discomfort
to jab out of me
all but
itself
Bent over, torso and face sweaty
my mind only fear
I wait, wish
this was not happening
that again all internal functions
were as feelingless, seamless
as
before
Surely this is the way the last breath
approaches:
the body become a bully
stridently insistent
enforcing its primacy over the brain
No wonder we hate the animal
in the Other: oblivion
of the self, flesh
more vulnerable than it knows
screeching its triumph
from a burning pyre

And the dark reversed image
of personality, too
is revealed
All the ordinary mind
gone in an instant:
the obsessive thought
I cannot function
—with the car not fixed

—in the absence of the person
  I love so much
—with these loud noises from next door
Or the chemical imbalance
when every hedge and twig
shouts warning, each encounter
with another human
means messages of threat
subtle, but decipherable,
and vital to interpret, to act on
if I am to
survive
The voice inside
my head
explaining, prodding
denouncing

My self
so fragile
in this mirror
What fire
or hammer
to smash it
protect me

Death's scythe
polished
to a gleaming
black
reflection

PRAISE

I

Praise
is
grass, rising everyplace
except in me
and other people
The frog has no anxiety
about what it is
neither has the squirrel
or nuthatch
or rose
They do not berate themselves
nor
forgive themselves
They are full of the confidence
we long for
look to other people to give us
and call
praise

II

"Praise God"
the saying goes
"Give God the glory"
The lyrics of the old mountain hymn
describe Heaven as where
we, together with angels, will
laud the deity
"forevermore"
This concept, then
sees even the Creator of All
insecure
needing eternal reassurance that
He or She is worthy

honoured
valued
Unless: this is metaphor
to do with the Kingdom within
(which presumably includes
its Star Attraction)
so what we are called
to praise
ceaselessly
is
our part in creation
(our portion of the
divine, if you like)
our
selves

III

Consider a world of praise
—not phony, but
where accurate praise is
part of everyday
given to others
received
constantly
Wouldn't that be
Heaven?

THE POLITICS OF THE HOUSE

THE POLITICS OF THE HOUSE: TABLES

Tables are egalitarians.
Each stands on its four legs
and whatever is placed on them—a sumptuous cloth
and silver cutlery
or a paper cover with plastic plates and spoons—
the table knows its purpose is the same.
Even the most exquisitely carved sort
are cautioned by their parents when young:
Never forget: take our chairs away from us
and all we are is a shelf.
But as long as we bear up
those objects we are asked to hold
we are each successfully doing our work in the world.

In this way tables are like horses:
indifferent to whether they carry a rich man
on an expensive saddle
or a young girl bareback, pull a plough
or a carriage of tourists. Certain kinds of horses
are best for specific jobs
but among horses themselves there are no hierarchies.
A Clydesdale believes itself as accomplished in its own way
as an Arabian, neither one deferring to
nor lording it over the other.

Unlike horses, though,
tables remain a sign of human civilization:
a central item of our houses—kitchen table,
sewing table—and our cities
—workbench, packing table.
Sadly, the men and women around the boardroom table
still imagine themselves worth more
than the women and men seated at the lunchroom tables
on their break. Yet in the midst

of all our ranking and gradations,
qualifications, certificates, and ornate hats,
tables
patiently continue to demonstrate
the ubiquitous nature of equality.

THE POLITICS OF THE HOUSE: CHAIRS

Any chair is a success
if it can support a woman or man

without collapsing.
Chairs may be padded, or bare, shaped wood,

foldable, stackable
or reclining. Yet each

in its prime is our ally:
who isn't thankful for

an opportunity to sit down?
Of course there are renegade chairs—

hard and uncomfortable
making a meeting, lecture

or even a dinner party
unendurable.

Also, there are office chairs
designed to be below the height

of one other person's chair in a room
to intimidate us,

to teach us what the owner of these chairs
thinks is our place.

Yet outlaw chairs
are the exception,

are in no way representative
of chairdom. Chairs are the essence

of what befriends us on this planet.
We travel greater distances in chairs,

for instance, than on beds
or even our own feet.

And although many of the tasks
we have to do to keep the world going

are performed standing up,
an enormous number get accomplished

while we are seated.
And other jobs could be:

after years of doctors trying to force us
to give birth on our backs, for example,

we have begun to return
to a more natural position—

using a birthing stool, the chair
of life. In fact, chairs adopt the atttitude

of the Earth toward humanity:
ever-present, neutral toward our individual achievements

but generally hospitable
to the endeavours of our species.

For these reasons
it is easy to comprehend why

some primitive tribes buried their dead
in a sitting position.

After all, if there is a life beyond this one,
probably in that existence, too,

more will have to be done seated
than stretched out—loafing or sleeping.

What does seem mysterious
is why none of these early peoples

developed a burial chair.
Such an object obviously would represent

a veneration owed the most useful human construct.
No doubt such artifacts are absent

because unlike weapons, pottery, jewelry
or anything else found in ancient graves

chairs are too valuable
to mail on to the next world.

The Politics of the House: Beds

Beds are close relatives to tables:
four legs that raise a level surface.
But beds are even more self-effacing
than their cousins, perhaps due
to beds' shorter stature.
When we refer to beds, we usually mean
not the physical construction
but the colour and weight of blankets
and the number or thickness of pillows.
Sometimes we have in mind how soft the mattress feels
or else a bedspread
that entirely hides the bed beneath it.

This imprecision in terms
affects young people in particular.
When they begin life on their own
they often decide: "I don't need a bed. I'll sleep
on a foam pad on the floor."
We discover the virtues of beds, however,
through their absence.
Not that any bed would take advantage
of our confusion. Like tables
they perform their function
with as little fuss as possible,
only objecting if under great stress
or very old.

Loyal to a fault, a bed will support
generation after generation
without complaint—no matter how often it hears
someone who merely tucked in the sheets
announce: "I made
the bed."

THE POLITICS OF THE HOUSE: SINKS

Sinks are the mouths of houses:
perpetually open, shining white
or metallic, running with a
necessary fluid.
Most people's sinks resemble most people's mouths:
never quite living up to the ideal images
in advertising, or to the fixtures of the rich
shown in movies. Most of us
display something slightly chipped or broken,
off centre,
that leaks a little
or contains, if you look closely,
little particles of food or
unidentifiable substances caught in tiny crevices.
Some people's sinks are
old and discolored
the way teeth can become: still serviceable
but worn and badly stained. From time to time
such a sink
is taken out and replaced. As with false teeth,
the substitute sink calls attention to itself
by its inappropriate perfection:
the new sink looks far less natural
than the one that honestly
served its house for so long.

THE POLITICS OF THE HOUSE: CURTAINS

Curtains are the clothing of windows.
A lack of these hanging pieces of
cloth or plastic
indicates nakedness—an untenanted space
waiting for its new appearance—or else
laundry day.
Like clothes, curtains say a lot about the wearer:
the diaphanous tease of sheers,
the sturdy functionality of bedroom drapes
aiming to stop all light, the cheerful colours
that brighten kitchens, the sly peek-a-boo
of Venetian blinds.

              Thus, viewed from outside,
curtains are signal flags
that provide the sailors who read them
with data about the vessels observed.
As well as whether a room is
occupied or unoccupied,
these pennants can inform about
the room's function, and the taste, heritage
or economic situation
of the ship's owners, or the people who
currently live aboard. Curtains can announce
whether the crew is awake and on watch
or below decks asleep.

Curtains' indication of so much
helps to explain why most spend their time
drooping from rods or hooks,
exhausted. Real flags at least
get to flap in the wind
and hence develop muscle tone
and usually a pugnacious nature.
And clothes have the opportunity
to tour around the house
—not to mention the globe. But curtains

just passively
impart their knowledge,
more familiar with dust than with open spaces,
like a travel poster conveying information
about a place it will never see.

THE POLITICS OF THE HOUSE: APPLIANCES

Like nurses
these were once dressed
only in white. Now the uniforms they wear,
like those of their human counterparts,
display a range of pastels.
But the function
of stoves, refrigerators,
clothes dryers
remains as before: to aid the body
to hygienically achieve
its renewals—to fuel itself,
to clean or restore
whatever is soiled or lacking.

Major appliances
with their practical assistants
—shavers, toasters, vacuum cleaners—
tangibly improve our health and ease.
But whereas flesh-and-blood nurses
can arrive where we are
to offer succour and solace
or carry out instructions prescribed by men and women
considered even more knowledgeable about our bodies,
we have to approach
mechanical devices
to receive their comfort.
Also, unlike a person, any household apparatus
contributes just a portion of the help we need or want.
Each must be visited
regularly and in turn.

For most of our existence
we require human nursing
only during comparatively brief
periods of illness.
But once we placed ourselves
in the care of appliances,

we signed into
a long-term facility
—to be nursed round-the-clock
for the remainder of our days.

THE POLITICS OF THE HOUSE: ALARM CLOCK

As soon as you are old enough
you are given or must buy
the smallest, most portable part
of a school, a factory,
or every place where
you are summoned, dismissed and otherwise given orders
with whistles and bells.

The rulers of these institutions
make it a requirement that you keep
this thermostat of the hours,
this mandatory tool
near at hand
and especially in the room where you are closest
to escaping their control:
where you stretch out
      make love
          dream

Long before electronic pagers
the alarm clock
linked us continually
to whoever bought and sold our time.
Like some household shrine
this instrument
receives our devotions twice daily during the workweek
—once when we set it, and again
when we shut it off.
Even on holidays
its presence reminds us of a power
greater than ourselves, than our wishes.
This is the sole domestic appliance
we each consider necessary to possess
yet regard with loathing.

I believe this device
constantly reveals
a sickness at the core of our lives:
what kind of social structure
needs these mechanical or electric cattle prods
in every house
in order to function?
Is no other way possible
to arrange the work of the world
without forcing us to board at our home
this pitiless timekeeper
        this company stooge
                this factory foreman
                from a century before?

THE POLITICS OF THE HOUSE: COUNTERS

A counter is
a cross between a shelf and a cabinet.
In stores, a counter frequently has a glass top
or front, to reveal what it contains.
But in a house, counters usually are opaque.
Their contents are secret,
put out of sight for now.

Whatever counters are like, though,
they have nothing to do with relaxation.
We ordinarily stand at a counter
—to work or buy.
When a restaurant offers counter service
it is for people who wish to eat in a rush
compared to the women and men who choose booths or tables.

And no kitchen anywhere
has enough counters.
Each kitchen displays the same motto
engraved on the air:
if the designer of this kitchen
had to cook in it
there would have been more counter space.
In my house, for instance, the fridge
is alongside one edge of the stove
and the only unoccupied nearby flat surface
is a narrow strip between the stove's other side
and the dish drainer.

One of the indisputable signs
that the Revolution has triumphed
will be a rearrangement of counters.

THE POLITICS OF THE HOUSE: THE ELEMENTS

I. WATER

Primary system
of a house: before the foundation is dug
water must be secured
—in the country, by water rights
or well; in the city
by an arrangement with the municipal authorities
to tap the main.

A house without water
is a great ship beached
above tide line
—like an aircraft
with engines inoperative
displayed in a museum: complete in every aspect
except its most essential.

And once water reaches the dwelling
it enters a maze of copper and brass,
of plastic, porcelain, stainless steel.
Ingenious and intricate structures
collect and distribute,
hold and release.
Plus, there are filters, valves, and other devices
that must be monitored
and repaired or replaced.
For although water consents to be led
into the factory of the home
to perform the tasks we set it,
water never abandons its self-respect:
its stubborn insistence on wearing down
everything it touches
and its curiosity—
or, as some label it,
obstinate tendency
to become distracted

—in whichever interpretation, its urge to discover
where each crack or even pinhole
in what intends to contain it
might lead.

2. HEAT

In the climates
I inhabit
much of the year a house needs
heat: a furnace in the basement
and registers or electric baseboards in each room.
In these months a dwelling lacking warmth
is as untenable for people
as an enclosure lacking oxygen.
If the heat for some reason fails
the inhabitants begin to don protective garments.
The longer the cold seeps into the building
the more those moving around inside
resemble hard-hat divers, astronauts outside their capsules
atomic workers in an irradiated environment
or anybody attempting to function
in an atmosphere without usable air.

3. ELECTRONS

Like fire, electrons are the servant class
of the house.
They provide us with amenities
that we quickly regard as necessary.
Electrons conceal within themselves
fire, as is evident when faulty wiring
or an overloaded electrical apparatus
suddenly releases the flames it hides.
Yet when we first brought electrons into buildings

we thought of them as water, not fire:
hence the complicated pathways for electricity
hidden within the walls
and electrical faucets conveniently located
at intervals around the periphery of each room.
But unlike water, we also allow cords
—the piping for electrons—
to tangle visibly at the edges of rugs
and the rest of our living space
in a manner we would never tolerate
if these were really hoses.
Whether such wires connect speakers
to a sound system, or a telephone
to its jack, or simply link a table lamp
to the nearest outlet
everyone pretends the cords aren't present.
Nobody ever comments, for instance,
"You did a nice job of plugging in the microwave oven."
Nor are there night school courses offered
on home wire arranging.
And yet our insistence on not seeing these cables
is a tribute to
the invisible nature of electrons themselves,
their secret fire.

4. STRUCTURE

Thoreau claims
a house is only an elaborate cover
built over a hole
in the earth: a basement
to him
is the fundamental structural element
of a human habitat.
To me
any structure is tied

109

to the ground, a construction
of the soil
no less than a vegetable
or flower.
However, as with these,
we usually cherish
—except for underground shopping malls
or edible roots like carrots
—what lifts into air,
filled with heat in season
and, always, water.
Such extrusions
from the earth
match our own being:
the planet's surface is what we stand on,
spread across, make use of,
recognize each other as occupying.
Only at the end of our lives
do we accept Thoreau's gap in the soil
as our residence
and even then, that which gets planted there
is no more ourselves
than are clothes or other grave-goods.
While we live, we anchor our structures
to the planet, keep one eye always
on the ground.
Earth is the base line
from which we start
and return, but in the meantime
we try to rise
to rise

SOME RANTS

SOLIDARITY

We go out to do it
believing if everybody did a little
nobody would have to do very much.
After a while we notice
hardly anyone is doing it.
Then the behavioural psychologists hasten forward
to point out that *because* we do it
no one else does.
Does this mean if we did less
others would do more?
Or that if nobody did it
everybody would do it?
Since we lack proof the latter is true, however,
we go out and do it.

THE WRECKERS

for "Rural Dignity"—opponents of the
Canadian government's elimination of many
country post offices and delivery routes

One morning, along the lake road
it was as though vandals had passed by in the dark
and torn each mailbox from its post
at the top of the gravel driveways
and then hammered the metal containers
flat on the ground.
Where the mail receptacles could not be ripped
away from their supports
the entire structure had been pulled over
before the metal was dented in.
And when we, one by one, showed up
at the village post office to request them to
hold our mail while we repaired the damage,
we found the small building gutted by fire:
the blackened boards still steaming
in the noon light.

　　　　　　　　We telephoned the police
to report our loss and to inquire
who could have done these things
and why. But the constable at the other end
sounded uneasy. *It was authorized,*
he said. Later we learned
this is what he told everybody,
yet at the time we were each staggered
by his statement. Disbelieving,
we attempted to obtain more details from him,
to argue. *That is all I can tell you,*
he said. *Any other information
will have to come from
your elected representative.*

But they, too,
were little help. Those men and women we voted for
who belong to the groups out of office
blame the ruling party for what happened, promising
if we change who has the majority
there is a good chance matters will improve
—as long as what we want is
fiscally responsible.
The women and men in power
seemed sympathetic at first,
blaming these unfortunate events on decisions by
post office management
they vowed to review
in the near future. But when we continued
to ask for assistance
these representatives
became sterner, said our attitude
is monetarily unwise. They announced to the media
country highways are more environmentally appealing
without the clutter of individual mailboxes
and hence their removal will increase tourism,
benefiting the entire community.
They proclaimed the village building
was not burned down
but spontaneously aged and decayed overnight.
They added that the wisdom
of the post office executives they appointed
will be evident in five or ten years
provided the new policies are given an opportunity to work,
and the resultant improved balance sheet
will demonstrate to every citizen
that those who oppose these measures
are misguided or
liars.

Yet as we listened to the speeches to reporters
and to the chambers and houses of legislation,

we noticed one noun
that flashes and sparkles
repeatedly among the statements and rebuttals,
two syllables
rolled lovingly around these tongues,
a word uttered with awe,
the way orators had once pronounced
God or *the people*. That cherished word
is *money*.
More significant than our needs
or wishes, this substance is invoked
to explain and defend
all these legislators
do. By how they speak the word,
it is obvious dollars are what they represent
in their assemblies: cash, not ourselves,
has elected them
to govern on behalf of cash;
they are the honourable members
from Money.

No wonder when we arrive before them
with our delegations and petitions
they appear resentful
and confused: we don't look like money,
we don't behave like money.
Why shouldn't they be anxious
to brush us aside
to meet with the real folks from home:
dollars?

Thus as we gather
to discuss among ourselves and create
from our lives—on ruins
other men and women have caused—
different values,

by such acts we sustain
a fragile concept
older than the first settlement
at the north end of this valley,
a belief that endures through poverty and better years.
Each time we together refuse
what diminishes us,
what those who rule us have ordered us to accept,
it is not only rural dignity we
struggle to give birth to and help grow,
but
human dignity.

THE HOUSE WITH THE BLUE ROOF

A man is hitting a child
in a room in my house
while a woman watches
—a woman whose mouth is sealed
by purple flesh

And in another room in
my house
three men are beating a fourth
Fists, boots
descend on that human body
coiled on a cement floor
Pain sears
like a jet of fire
as each blow strikes

> There is also a room
> where a baby frowns
> with absolute concentration
> as she takes her first steps
> from one pair of laughing hands
> to another

In my house
are rooms
across which someone has strung barbed wire
and steel constructions
from wall to wall
Young boys with guns
and a vacant stare
stand next to a small opening in this fence

while in a different room
a bulldozer
is burying corn
near bags of burning rice
Along the corridor
an assembly hall

is filled with lines of skeletal forms
whose hands clutch empty metal bowls

This happens
under the single blue roof
of my house

And it is
my house
—each room
mine, even though some person within
driven mad by circumstances
screeches threats
at me, or has seized the power
to hurt me
or those I love
or hate

There is a room
all summer garden:
the sounds of birds
and insects
busy among the
hot green leaves

And a room entirely of stumps
the scorched soil around them
thinning into mud, flowing away
below each downpour

—such weather
one of many ceilings
under the roof

of my house
the solitary roof
of my house
my house

THEY MADE MY CITY INTO TWO CITIES

Vancouver

They made my city into two cities
I was watching but they did it anyway
One city with the sea breeze pouring up
through the clean streets
shadowed by enormous chestnut and cedar trees
under which are expensive boutiques and restaurants
houses costing so much you feel unworthy just looking at them
And down at the harbor, marinas full of boats priced
almost as high as the houses
with pennants flying gaily from masts
and from the balconies of taverns, import shops
and even food markets
catering exclusively to the rich
And to the east
is the other city
sidewalks cracked and patched
the trees spindly, discount merchandise for sale
and no ocean
except an industrial waterfront
vigilantly protected by the Ports police:
grain elevators, fish canneries, warehouses
with fences and railroad yards to keep you
as distant as possible from what might have been beaches
The avenues are stifling, if it isn't raining
the bars jammed and smoky
and, outside, the buses drag us from place to place
looking for work, like defective goods
being offered as joblots to various junk dealers
Even the mountains to the north, that on the west side
sparkle beautifully
here look vaguely menacing, like a health care premium increase
or a cut in welfare
The massive peaks seem like duties or procedures
we're going to have to fulfil
to stay out of jail

Wait just a minute, I can hear you saying
Weren't there always two cities?
And who are the "they" you're blaming
again for the world's troubles?

Yes, there were always two cities: the wealthy and the poor
But I grew up here, and don't remember
the gap so large
I don't recall businesses like the take-out Italian restaurant
that announced they would not deliver east of Main
or the monthly magazine issued by the largest newspaper
distributed only to the western half of my city
(You should have read the paper's consumer columnist
justifying this—how we'd all benefit
since the increased revenues would result in an improved daily product
even for east enders, blah blah blah)
There was certainly a ritzy neighbourhood or two
but I don't remember the quarantining of so many districts
to eliminate anyone not rolling in money
as inflated house prices result
in only a tiny percentage of human beings
being able to live there
I don't remember this situation
encouraging real estate profiteers
to demolish what cheaper dwellings survive in every neighbourhood
and to replace them with staggeringly expensive apartments and homes
I know back then a swath was never cut through the east side
to build a little toy elevated train
that now delivers we slaves to our downtown jobs faster
(since house costs have forced us to live further and further from work)
Somebody kept insisting how wonderful this elevated system
was going to be, though they had to trash the bus service
to get enough of us to ride on it
to justify its existence
and a special tax had to be added onto both gasoline
and our electricity bill
to help subsidize such a marvel

121

Best of all were the cries of outrage
that went up from the west side
when it was proposed the little train should cut through
their neighbourhoods
to connect with a suburb to the south into which
more of us had been pushed
"Not on your life!" the howl went up.
"Who do you think we are? *Who*
do you think we are?"

And that question brings us to your other point:
who *are* the "they"
that tore my city into two
(and who, as far as I can tell,
would be happy if they could eradicate the poorer half entirely
leaving this place restricted to the well-heeled)?
This is a question that's bothered me most of my life:
who decided that those who own an enterprise
should get more money than the rest of us who work at it each day?
I'm not talking about the wage structure, understand
I know each of us can construct dozens of excuses
why we should be paid more than the women or men working
        alongside us
No problem there (though this is what helps keep
the majority of us earning a lot less than we could be)
I'm talking about *decisions*: who, and how was it, determined
my city should be two cities?

Some people blame it on offshore money:
Japanese yen with nowhere else to be spent
Hong Kong dollars that have to be extracted from the colony
before the Chinese government at last reclaims
what belongs to its people
On the east side, graffiti expresses this viewpoint
with the area's usual delicate regard for personal feelings:
"Chinks hired? You're fired!"
the walls say. On the west side, the matter

122

is handled a little differently
such as when the federal government gave the Bank of Hong Kong
five million dollars "to financially assist"
their purchase of the Bank of B.C.
Such solidarity among the wealthy
—sharing around the trough of public money
for their own profit—regardless of skin colour
or national origin
maybe expresses a healthier outlook, however,
than ours
For aren't we all immigrants
except for the tribes we hurt so viciously?
How can we draw a line and say:
"Now that I'm here, everybody else who arrives
is an alien life form"?
In any case, for every overseas arrival who buys in
somebody local must have sold out
Are the latter folks, then, the elusive "they"
I want to blame?
I observe how men and women from the other city
keep showing up where we live
to try to talk land prices higher and higher
and to convince people to open upscale catering enterprises
only a few blocks from the Food Bank lines
Probably the next step will be to operate charter bus tours
to bring tourists to watch our frenzies on Cheque Day
which some west-siders like to regard as
a sort of Carnival
and which I'm sure the provincial Ministry of Tourism
would like to see expanded
into parades, floats, street dances
a monthly Mardi Gras
instead of shouting and glass breaking in the street
tires screeching, people staggering blankly around
or being sick on the sidewalk
falling down, or lurching past bleeding
from a skinned forehead and cut knuckles

or with eyes blackened and a broken nose
being hauled into wagons by the cops
or directed by social workers to an already-full women's shelter

Now if you think we're not getting too far
in determining who so transformed my city
maybe I can rephrase the issue:

why should there be
some men and women with too much money
and others with not enough?
Why isn't wealth, in a rich province
shared more equally? Can't we figure out
how to redistribute what we all help earn
or is it that we don't want to?
Anyway, why should the gulf between the cities
get wider and wider? Where do we go
if we can't afford to live in our neighbourhood any longer?
Why should we have to leave?

Gee, this is like a quiz
Twenty-five points for each right answer!
And if nobody can come up with the correct response
I'll finish with a few additional questions:

what's wrong with there being one city of the very well off
and one of the increasingly poor?
Who has the power to change it?
Who *should* have the power to change it?
How do we stop
what's happening to us?

THE LIE

A lie does not solve a problem
regardless of how often
the lie is retold.
Each lie expands the difficulty
it was meant to conceal or solve,
transforming the situation into more
shapes and layers. Each new complexity
bloats, enlarging and gaining weight.

And to tell a lie
is to open a can of patching tar,
lift out a daub of the black, viscous material
with a putty knife,
then smear it
on the chest of the person you lie to.
From your viewpoint, perhaps this individual looks stupid
standing talking
with a blob of runny goo on their shirt
they aren't yet aware of.
In some cases, the stain you have created
can be laundered out.
If the lie is serious, though,
you will have destroyed this article of their clothing.
They are unable now ever to present themselves
entirely as they did before you lied to them.

But you must be careful
how you grasp the container of tar.
The substance tends to ooze over the rim
onto the fingers,
just as a too-vigorous application of the tar
will leave spots on your other hand and wrist.

Also, if you have to tell lies constantly
—either for a living
or because no single lie
can rectify an error or damage—

an increasing amount of your exposed flesh
and your clothes
will be flecked with globs of tar.
Such spatters are difficult to scrub away
and will, despite attempts to remove them,
eventually merge,
visible to all.

        Worse, once enough tar
has accumulated on your skin,
acids and oils found in the human epidermis
react chemically
with the foreign matter.
The effects of this are most evident
in the face: lies
cause the cheeks to
sag; the black
works into crevices and lines,
deepening them.
Your face now indelibly appears
sullen and
wasted.

On The Planet of Adolescents

On the planet of adolescents
we spend our hours

waiting for the grown-ups to wake
and properly begin the day

To fill the time, we fall back further
to our childhood, and pretend:

"Say we're old enough to run things
Say we're grown

Say we're married
Say we're off to work

Say we've got our own business
Say we're in the Army

Say it's okay if we kill
Say it's okay if we steal

Say there's a god somewhere
who if you don't do all I say

will punish you eternally"

But there is no Papa in the sky
No Mama in the earth

There are only ourselves
who eye our brothers and sisters suspiciously

who want love
who won't share

who grab
who hit

who wish the others
wouldn't be so mean

X-Rated

THE LOVES OF THE PENIS

The penis is blind, and
nods through its ordinary hours
feeling like a drain spout,
an appendix, a mouth
with only one thing to say.
No wonder whenever, due to circumstances
out of its control
blood suddenly rushes to it
as though messengers are bringing vital news
to a person of importance,
the penis perks right up.
Sightless or not, it rears its head
like a business executive or captain
inspecting what he rules.
However, as with individuals who have spent
much time alone,
the penis is susceptible to such attention
and to flattery. Also, like everything blind
it has a developed sense of touch
and responds inappropriately to
affectionate gestures that involve
even slight physical contact.

In gratitude for any notice,
for being singled out,
the penis falls in love too easily
—like a puppy eager to please,
eager for a home.
As might be expected
of someone who not only cannot see
but is emotionally vulnerable, the penis
is not very discriminating
about its amours.
Even experience
appears to teach it nothing.
After a period of solitude
or unhappiness

it loses nearly all sense of judgement.
Like an addict, or anybody who depends
on external stimulus for
self-validation, it forgets
the unpleasant consequences
of its previous compulsive behaviours
and leaps at the chance
once more, for love.

One World Shutting Out Another

In the dark, the waves of the ocean
thrust against the beach
confidently, steadily,
the sibilance of water
pushing against shore
hides the small night sounds
of the city, the forest
So when the motion
at intervals
subsides
there is a tense
quiet
—a spell lifted
for some moments
and then resumed

>At the ends of my fingers
>tiny mouths
>open in the pads of flesh:
>mouths that begin to kiss
>whatever the tips of my hands
>touch
>down her neck
>to the base of the throat
>the outer edge and shape
>of each breast
>the thick sturdiness
>of the nipple
>
>and around the well
>of her navel
>where the body curves inwards
>to the place she once was tied
>to her mother—
>life-water
>circling to its
>start

as other of my tiny mouths
drink
from the fluid
flowing through the porous lagoon wall
in the moist
dim cavern
The sea inside us
now at high tide

I pull about me
flesh constructed of
water
that glows a fiery red-orange
in its softness

when I press my face into it
all vision, thought
ceases
in the neon warmth
floating around my skin

        myself
           no-self

    a slow luminous

    pulse

THIRD WATER

A drop of water
on the flattened needle
of a hemlock

      Rain
      falling steadily in the forest air
      so as I kiss her beautiful face
      I can tongue water away
      from skin smooth and taut as water
      and seconds later, when we kiss again
      her cheek is slick once more

      as though this moisture
      arose from within her
      the way a mountain puts forth
      a towering waterfall
      —high above the valley floor
      enough runoff has gathered
      to descend all year
      in a continual flow

      yet if her water is internal
      its chill and buoyancy
      make it almost another substance
      than the hot liquid that pours
      from her back and her thighs
      as she twists with love

I do not think I will choose this coolness
nor the heated other
and certainly not the dust
that thickens the corners and bends
of my calendar's numbers:
that suffocating dust
panic's ally, the fuzzy coating
on lettuce or celery
left too long in a referigerator

a haze of blue circles on the bread
or cheese

There is a third water
I seek
I have never seen

        This in an age
        where men and women are building crates
        to ship the water, to sell it

        far to the south

        And once this water is drunk
        those who consume it will follow its passage
        north, they cannot help themselves
        they must migrate
        homing
        to the source here, these creeks
        rushing across the mountain stones

Perhaps this third water
is found in a kernel of valley corn
or in the eye of a crow
or within the tiny pool
hanging on the tip
of a hemlock needle

        not surplus water
        but water altered—a drier water
        wetter dust:
        love
        distilled from the moist air
        of these woods
        from particles
        of damp forest soil
        the clear water
        bearing down her hot face

THE WINLAW ELEGIES

THE WINLAW ELEGIES

Winlaw, in heavy rain
Down country roads, the May leaves
have burst out on stems and branches
In a flower bed, below early tulips
the blade of a gladiolus
breaks the surface
like the dorsal fin of a shark

This past twelvemonth, the earth received
more of my dead
From the moment they were born, this is the only Spring
they have not seen
—along the lane, the hillsides
choked with alder
and the underbrush's puffs of blossoms
floating through the steadily falling water

The trees, weeds, grass stalks
push out of the soaked ground
with as much haste as they can
as though they shared our species' repugnance
for lying still, covered with soil
Each green flag is an affirmation, a cry of joy
long live the living
Each a perfect elegy
for what remains in the damp dark
for what goes under
and does not return

MOUNTAIN ELEGY

Dave Bostock

Late on the day of his death,
high in the alpine
above the trees, I crossed a field
more stone than earth
and found what I had climbed for.
Where ice and the cold
pummel the hard ground,
where frost and the relentless glacial wind
tear at whatever tries to live,
the moss campion
adheres to bits of soil
lichens have generated over eons
from rock. The campion, too,
has infinite patience:
a decade passes
before it will flower.
After a quarter-century
it spreads no wider
than the outstretched fingers of a hand.
But the flower digs in, buffeted by the nightly chill,
by solar rays, by hail, the Spring melt,
smothered for much of the year beneath snow.
Air trapped in its leaves
and clusters, however,
forms a minute protected place
out of the wind and
warmed by sun.
Here, other plants are born
and nurtured.

> His laughter
> was such an enclosure
> in the roaring life below.
> *One time I'd been working welding*
> *on a logging show in the Charlottes.*

I had a couple of grand saved
so decided to quit. This was when
if you had any kind of trade, any kind of ticket
you were in demand.
It was no big deal to change jobs.
On Friday
I picked up my pay, and made a point
of finding the boss
and telling him exactly, in detail,
what I thought of him
and where he could put
the whole outfit. Then I was on the plane
for Rupert, with some of the other guys.
We'd already had plenty to drink
before we even got on board.

On Monday I woke up
in the Rupert Hotel.
I had no idea
how I had spent the weekend
but I discovered I was absolutely broke.
Every cent of my two thousand dollars was gone.
I phoned to the camp I just left
and asked if I could have my job back.
"Sure, Dave," the boss said.
"Report as soon as you get in."
"Uh, Mr. Johnson?" I had to say.
"Could you advance me the money
for the plane? I don't have
quite enough to cover the fare."
"Okay," he said. That's how it was at the time:
tear a strip off 'em on Friday
and grovel on Monday
and they'd rehire you.
It was special. Try that today, though,
and see how far you get.

I camped that night
just above treeline, by a cluster of dwarf firs,
a *krumholz*, formed on the barren
by a single plant
whose roots tunnel upslope
and emerge, or whose branches
pushed down by snow
take root. Such gatherings, too,
create within themselves
an eddy of more hospitable weather
in the high, harsh air.
These conifer islands are also how trees advance,
pushing toward the summit: forerunners
marking and clearing a path
others will follow in relative certainty
and ease.

> *I had a job with a pile-driving crew*
> *—metal piles. The company was Ontario-based*
> *and I think this was the first time*
> *they had hired union labour.*
> *Anyway, one of their foremen*
> *was forever showing up to order you to do*
> *some task you'd already begun.*
> *I'd have finished a weld*
> *and was packing up my gear to move*
> *to the next spot, when the foreman would come by*
> *and say: "Dave, I want you to pack your equipment*
> *and haul it over there for the next weld."*
> *For a time this guy only seemed silly*
> *but one morning—I don't know, it was a bad day*
> *or something—he really started to bother me.*
> *When for the nine-hundredth time*
> *the foreman ordered me to start*
> *what I already was in the middle of,*
> *I lost it. I began to whine, real loud:*
> *"Aww, you're always telling me*
> *to do that. I don't wanna. Why do I*

have to go down in that hole
and weld? How come you don't tell
anybody else to do it?"
The foreman's face went white.
He didn't know what to say.
He backed off, but others on the crew had heard
and a few minutes later I heard a whine
from over by the crane:
"I don't wanna do that. You're always
saying I have to. How come I
have to be the one to do it?"
After this, there was no stopping the guys.
All over the site, whenever the foreman
tried to tell anybody anything
you'd hear this incredible whining:
"Awww. I don't wanna." Afterwards, we called it
a whine-in. The foreman
only lasted a couple more days
then he was gone.

The heat of my fire
slashes at my face
when I bend to lever
a log further into the flames.
The song of his life—his work,
his music, his joy—
brought him a cancer that spread
through his body, shrunken
beyond remedy, and then the pneumonia
he chose
to let kill him.
From the peaks around me in the dark,
wind and sun and the earth's turning
bring the snowpack
to the valleys we dwell in
—whether as water
or cold air

we breathe, and then we don't breathe,
leaving behind
our laughter or rage,
our unfinished stories
whispered toward the stars.

FIRE ELEGY

Bron Wallace

How strange that an entire person
has become
ash

to be poured
into winter wind

To me, she still listens
to a point I'm making as we talk
her lit cigarette held away from
the corner of her mouth
Then she places the cigarette
in a saucer and stands up
and walks into another room
to find a book to show me
why I'm wrong

          Her voice stops
as she searches
in a different part of the house
In her kitchen
are only the sounds from the street
I watch smoke
twist upward from a cylinder
burning among stubbed ends
of ones she breathed in from
earlier

Or she is
the faint smell of such smoke
that lingers for days in my house
after a party, or a visit by certain friends

Even if I open doors, windows
to let in new air
a trace of that odour
hovers

What I sense now
of her
in every room

RIVER ELEGY

Leo Clavir

On an autumn day, I worked the canoe
upstream
to a pool by one shore
where a cottonwood shades
a back eddy. Fish
live here, that can be seen
below the hull.
But when I leaned
to watch
I stood at another river's edge
under these waters
on an afternoon like this afternoon
of valley mist
and stillness.

As in the world above
the river was low:
its surface betrayed few traces
of the current.
Then Leo was
beside me.
"Leo?" I asked
after a moment,
amazed at my level tone.
He nodded.
Another pause. "Is this
where you live now?"
I said.
His hands lifted, palms up
in his familiar shrug.
This is it,
he replied, his voice as ever
a mix of assertion and humour,
ready for his wry laugh.
Nearby grew trees and bushes

of types I didn't recognize.
Through the thin fog
I could see odder forms of greenery
on the opposite bank.

"What's it like here?"
I blurted. "Are you alone,
or can you meet with friends?
What do you do all day, or are there
days and nights in this place?"
His face became serious.
I haven't left the earth
just because I don't get up
and put my pants on in the morning.
I exist as long as I'm part
of those who knew me.
I can be anywhere they are.
I'm also with the others
I knew who died
but, he grinned, *I'm not with them, too.*
He gave his shrug again.
Don't worry if you don't get it.
I'm not sure I understand it all myself.
For instance, in this spot it's not exactly
day or *night.*

"But can you work at things?"
I asked. He looked puzzled.
"You always used to have schemes
underway," I explained. "Can you influence
what happens to you
or what occurs around you?"
I pointed at the river.
"This water is flowing,"
I said. "So there must still be time
in this place, right?
The river must end somewhere

and take a certain while to arrive.
If nature can cause change like this,
how about people?"

You're not entirely
accurate,
he said slowly.
This river isn't quite a river
though the difference isn't easy to describe.
More like a metaphor
you really live in.

And then I was him
as a young man, striding up the hill
above a truckers' cafe
where a driver promised me a ride to New York
if I waited along the road
I was hitching south
fifty dollars in my pocket
to arrange the first distribution
of the new Soviet films
into Canada, already planning
where we would present them in Toronto
and how we could take them on tour
to the mining camps up north

And my body was also aged forty more years
climbing the steps of an Edmonton TV station
to promote our new shows
I was moving gingerly, watching for ice,
only recently out of hospital
after my heart attack

I struggled
to earn a good living,
Leo was saying,
and to try to create a better world.

149

The greatest delight for me
—though it's also a royal pain in the neck—
is to make life more enjoyable
not only for yourself
but everyone you share the planet with.
Myself, my wife,
my companions
including your parents,
we held up the lantern
and took a step. We thought the journey
would be brief
and at the start we were sure
there was just one possible road.
Now it's obvious
the path is far lengthier
and not as clear
as we imagined.
Yet it's no less important
to keep walking.

We listened
to the river.
"But are you happy
with this place," I asked,
"with how you're treated, for example?"
So, who's ever happy? Leo said, smiling.
I had lots of pleasure
but plenty of trouble, too,
where I used to exist.
As for here, and I noticed the fog around us
had thickened; it was difficult to see
much beyond him,
I'm both glad and not so glad
about the amount I can accomplish,
with being hidden in time.
When I speak, it can only be
to those who are alive. The swirls of mist

had become dense enough
that the outline of his body
was beginning to cloud,
yet his voice was strong:
Keep going. If you're right
in what you attempt,
you're right,
even if I might have disagreed with you.
And if you're not...
I observed the fog waft upwards
near where his shoulders had been,
and knew he had shrugged,
When people get discouraged
and sit down where they are
nothing stirs, we all halt.
Only if that happens
will everything I wanted to achieve
be lost.

For an instant
I felt alone
deep in the mist,

then I was afloat again
paddle in hand
on the ordinary river

the rest of my day stretching out
ahead.

MY OLD MASTER

Earle Birney

When my old master grew even more ancient
he climbed a tree.
"What are you doing up there?"
people on the ground yelled at him.
"I'm going to pick an apple
for my love," my master called over his shoulder,
not pausing in his ascent.
"I want to re-enact the story in the Bible
the way it actually took place:
the man
gave Eve her apple."
"Nonsense," people shouted at his back.
"But even if it was true,
there is plenty of fruit
you can reach safely from the ground."
"I've seen those," my master said
as he clambered higher.
"They won't do for her.
I have to find her something faultless."
"You are far too elderly
to be fooling around in trees,"
the people below screeched at him.
"Come down this instant."
"Love is never old," my master replied,
his voice only faintly audible.
His lanky, bony legs
were nearly out of sight.

Then he was gone.
Those standing under the tree
looked at each other and shook their heads.
"No fool like..." one said,
not needing to finish the sentence
since the others already were nodding agreement.
"If a terrible accident happens
it will just serve him right," another said.

A pattering of applause
endorsed this statement.

As if on cue
from high above
they heard a crash
and the ripping of foliage.
"Now he's done it," somebody on the ground said
with great satisfaction.
Indeed, after a minute or two
they could begin to make out in the topmost part of the tree
the body of my old master
bouncing and
spinning and rebounding
apparently out of control
as he fell through the branches.

But to my old master, the sensations he was experiencing
were not as awful as those below him
hoped and feared.
"For some reason, this tree
has taken off like a rocket
leaving me suspended in midair,"
my master observed to himself as he travelled
now upright, now head over heels.
"This is more than a little thrilling
except I'm being beaten black and blue
by the limbs flying past.
Lucky I got as far as I did
before this extraordinary event occurred."
And sure enough, in a few more minutes
the watchers on the ground could see
that whatever position his body assumed
in its tumbling, painful descent
my old master continued to grin triumphantly
as he clutched in his outstretched hand
a perfect apple.

In The Spirit

In the spirit, the body
flexes with the ease of hands
freed after hours within coarse gloves
or of feet
taken from heavy boots tipped with steel
In the spirit, the being
ripples like surfaces of light, of
water, like steam
rising from a lake, a stir of wind
that breathes
on that steam
In the spirit

>   we do nothing
>   but are everything
>   are created
>   but create nothing

what we were dissipates
like pollen
drifting back to the stars
while the spirit
gathers and
flows
A word
we knew was in us
but barely, scarcely heard
now vibrates
and we become
that sound
that meaning

in the spirit

EYE MOUNTAINS

The dead returned
have mountains
in their eyes
These dead watch the wind
know the reason
the aspen leaf shimmers
judge how well a crow
climbs up the thermals
hear what minnows listen to
as spring runoff
oozes into the water meadow
feel the stresses of the rocks
where one ridge leans away
The dead cherish blue-green puddles
on a dirt road
under a fresh sky
The dead
   Eyes
     Mountains

THE ASTONISHING WEIGHT OF THE DEAD

I am amazed
by the heaviness of the dead.
Whenever a dozen or so
of my dead are
seated around my front room
the cushions of the sofa and chairs
sink
under them, as if they lived.
These gatherings
like a small party
bring together those previously acquainted
and those from very distant
parts of my life.
At the first of these occasions
I was nervous some wouldn't get along.
But although death has preserved
the shape and gestures of their bodies
as well as the core of their
personalities, all seemed in a mood
to be amiable.
At the start, however, I tried anxiously
to keep conversation flowing,
to introduce Dave, for example, with his wonderful stories
to Joan, of the bright humorous eyes.
Where I saw two aunts from opposite sides of the family
who vaguely knew each other
chatting, I made a point of drawing in
Henrietta, who was about their age
and who I felt they'd enjoy.
But my twitching from group to group
was not needed—a hum of measured talk
rose from everyplace
along with laughter.
All were speaking pleasantly together
and at times one would rise
and cross the room to attach herself or himself
to a different twosome or threesome.

No one subservient
or boasting, each expressing in word and posture
the quiet confidence of
the vanished, present at my house
of an evening.
And the carpet
in its pile the next day
carries the imprint of their passages
and where they sat
or sprawled:
testimony
to the weight
of the astonishing dead.

THE GRAVE OF LITERARY AMBITION

I was planting bulbs on the grave
where literary ambition
is buried. Why not, I reasoned,
honour with beauty
the final resting place
of the friend/enemy
who sustained me for years?
I dug a shallow trench
and placed clusters of daffodils
and then tulips: each of these bulbs
the size and feel of a cooking onion.
Next I sowed crocuses, to provide a contrasting
purple shade
below the higher-stemmed, brighter flowers.
Then I sifted soil
to cover what I planted
and as the instructions on the bulb packages advised
watered thoroughly
and spread a coating of leaves for mulch.

But as I gathered
my shovel and rake and hoses
and was putting them in the wheelbarrow
I noticed a green shoot
poking through the brown layer of leaves.
"Must be the unseasonal weather,
warm for November,"
I thought, "or else my old ambition
is a powerful fertilizer.
Of course, maybe one bulb
is a hyperactive mutant."
Before I could trundle the barrow away,
however, another shoot appeared. And a third.
Suddenly dozens were springing up
everywhere on the low mound.
And the first one
already was producing

a tightly furled growth at its tip.
Within about a minute,
as more green spear-points
stabbed upward amid the leaves,
it unfolded a gorgeous,
multi-hued,
petal-soft
letter A.
Seconds later, more flower-letters
opened—not in any particular order—
to the autumn breeze
until the grave was transformed into a swaying,
iridescent
alphabet soup
lifted atop thick stalks.

Then the growth ended.
The letters waited
under a grey sky.
I picked a number of consonants and vowels
at random
and after I returned my gardening tools to the shed
I stuck the letters in a vase on my desk.

When I look up from my pen
or keyboard
here they are. Yet at idle moments
I catch myself starting a list
of words
that can be formed from these flowers.

THE ROCKIES: MAIN RANGE

Sundown
and polar cold
East of a white highway
on which my car
bucks against the icy wind
a ridge of peaks
—glacial
teeth of the Earth—
glow
in the last brightness of sky
The road is shadow, but
the line
of high frozen stones
incandesces
with intense, perfect snow
This splendour
belongs to another order
than the responses of men and women
as if the planet means to display
such glory
for its own appreciation
or for intelligences
existing prior to, or after
humankind
These crests
are alive, as the Earth is alive
and also dead beyond memory
like the rock now under the ground
The tiny car
passes far below
while the peaks stand
huge and
fragile
present briefly as the globe itself

as winter
as light

WALEY, WALEY

The boat will drift the last distance
to the dock
and I will climb out
and smell again
the pine forest along this side of the river
and the sweet woodsmoke
of the village chimneys.
At the front of the small crowd
waiting for me
is my wife, my bride,
with my young son in her arms
and Rachel, my daughter, peering
from behind her.
Then we are embracing,
and me awkward with the boy,
he squirming, Rachel shy, withdrawing.
But my friends
press around us
shouts of joy,
and laughter.
There are many present I thought
I would never greet again
—Dennis, with a witty quip
I only half hear, but no mistaking
his hug, Dave joking as before,
"Glad to meet you,
partner," handshake,
others, too, everyone excited with
bits of conversation
crossing and being misunderstood
and corrected with hilarity
and inquiries after missing friends.
Then we are all walking
the street, the log and plank houses
of the village
little changed from my memory of them,
people I don't know coming to doors and windows
to watch us pass, calling out,

members in our group bantering back,
laughing, Dennis says: "It's almost a parade."
"A procession!"
a voice at the rear cries.
And she walking beside me
her hand in mine, the flesh
soft and tight and familiar.
We enter the yard
of the rough wood synagogue
where the rabbi has come to the porch door
to receive us. I stand a pace or two from the others
alone before him
for his blessing,
his lined face hardly aged
as he leads the prayers.
Something tugs at my fingers:
Rachel has darted forward
to seize my hand, watching the ground
but holding fast. The small crowd thins
when we turn back to the street,
dispersing into the smoky evening
with promises to meet tomorrow.
The four of us
my family
journey a little further to the old house
and enter.

She moves through the rooms
arranging supper
and settling the children
while I watch: amazed to be once more
inside these walls, under these roof beams,
crossing these wood floors.
She shows me the newest
domestic changes: cloth she has woven
for the table, a new bench
by a window. And the latest
domestic problems: a sticking door latch,

where water is seeping around a fixture.
As of old, I begin to plan
how to tackle these,
the steady decay and resurrection of this house,
of any house, a rhythm I did not know I missed.
And then the meal, and the baby to bed,
and going in with her to Rachel,
and Rachel asking,
when I bend to kiss her,
"Will you be here in the morning?"
And I say: "Every morning. Now."
And Rachel turning over drowsily
under her covers.
Then seeing to the house lights,
suddenly awkward with each other,
the bedspread aglow in the last soft flame.

I waken deep in the blackness
and lie listening to the silences
of the house, its breathing
and creaks.
As carefully as possible
I swing my legs out
and stand naked in the room.
I move to the window
and shift the curtain,
looking out at the ridge
that rises to the west behind us,
its trees darker shapes
in darkness.
It is very late
yet I notice a light where Larry, the closest neighbour,
has come outside to shiver at the stars.
Perhaps the opening of the curtain
caught his eye: his face, lit by his open door,
swings to face this house, and he waves,
waves a welcome.
He points upwards, to remind me, perhaps,

of his old habit of checking the stars,
then he shrugs and goes in. The hour, the river beyond
the village, the forested mountain
are mine.

When I turn from the window,
her eyes, bright with love,
are watching me. We smile at each other.
A moment later I will be back in bed,
sharing a final kiss
before sinking into the warm
eternal
night.